Your Future as an AUTO MECHANIC

HIGH-DEMAND CAREERS™

Your Future as an AUTO MECHANIC

RACHEL GIVEN-WILSON AND TAMRA B. ORR

Rosen YA™
New York

Published in 2020 by The Rosen Publishing Group, Inc.
29 East 21st Street, New York, NY 10010

First Edition

Library of Congress Cataloging-in-Publication Data

Names: Given-Wilson, Rachel, author. | Orr, Tamra, author.
Title: Your future as an auto mechanic / Rachel Given-Wilson and Tamra B. Orr.
Description: First edition. | New York, NY : The Rosen Publishing Group, Inc., 2020. | Series: High-Demand Careers | Includes bibliographical references and index. | Audience: Grades 7–12.
Identifiers: LCCN 2018042728| ISBN 9781508187714 (library bound) | ISBN 9781508187707 (pbk.)
Subjects: LCSH: Automobiles—Maintenance and repair—Vocational guidance—Juvenile literature.
Classification: LCC TL152 .G528 2020 | DDC 629.28/7202—dc23
LC record available at https://lccn.loc.gov/2018042728

Manufactured in the United States of America

Contents

Introduction

Ever since the invention of the first car in 1886, there has been a need for qualified and skilled auto mechanics—also known as service technicians—to inspect, maintain, and repair these vehicles. Most Americans rely on their cars to get to work and school and to run basic errands, so when a car breaks down, it's usually a priority to get it fixed ASAP. That's where auto mechanics come in. Trained to diagnose problems with vehicles and figure out how to fix them, auto service technicians are invaluable in a car-driven society.

The field of auto mechanics is changing rapidly, but there are still plenty of jobs out there for skilled technicians who enjoy figuring out how things work.

Over the years, as auto technology has advanced, the job of diagnosing and fixing problems with vehicles has become more complicated. What was once seen as a "dirty job" is now often done on laptops in an office and requires advanced knowledge of computer systems. As customers and car manufacturers strive to make vehicles that are more environmentally friendly, the industry has seen a shift toward engines powered by alternative fuels. Moreover, with increasing numbers of electric vehicles (EVs) on the road, and the technology of self-driving cars advancing rapidly, the day-to-day work of auto mechanics continues to develop and change.

Joe Sevart began working in his father's auto service shop at the age of fourteen. Four decades later, he now runs the company, I-70 Auto Service in Kansas City, Missouri. Sevart told *The Atlantic* in a 2016 interview:

> I don't know if there's an industry that changes as rapidly as the automotive industry. Here we are, with the autonomous car; we've got cars that are out on the roads driving themselves with cameras in the back of the vehicles to make sure that we don't hit something backing up. We've got cars that are applying the brakes, because the human brain's not functioning quite fast enough. We have to adapt and change, and we've got to be educated.

Although cars and other motorized vehicles have changed dramatically over the years, the need for skilled auto mechanics continues to grow. Most professions suffer when the economy goes through a recession, but the maintenance and repair of engines and other equipment remains in demand, even when money is tight. During good economic times, consumers buy new equipment that requires regular maintenance and occasional repair. During harder economic times, they want to keep their vehicles in good working condition so they won't have to replace them. As a result, there is always a need for auto mechanics.

If you are considering a career as an auto mechanic, you should know that the industry is full of exciting opportunities and possibilities for specialization. Do you like to take things apart, figure out how they work, and put them back together? If you don't mind getting your hands dirty, you enjoy working with hand tools, and you love learning to use the latest computer and electronics systems, the field of auto mechanics could be a great career choice for you. And you don't have to wait until you're in college. There are plenty of things you can start doing now to get a head start in your chosen career!

Chapter 1

WHAT DOES IT TAKE TO BE AN AUTO MECHANIC?

The work of an auto mechanic often includes identifying problems with a vehicle, testing vehicle parts, and making sure all critical parts of the vehicle are examined. It also involves doing basic maintenance work, such as changing the oil, rotating the tires, and checking the fluid levels. When necessary, auto mechanics fix or replace parts of the vehicle that are worn, such as the brake pads or wheel sensors. Also, an important part of the job involves communicating with customers—clearly explaining the problems and the necessary repairs.

Some auto mechanics service and repair a vehicle's mechanical and electrical parts, while others focus on vehicle body repair or refinishing. Some focus on working with specific types of vehicles, such as heavy trucks or high-performance vehicles. As an auto mechanic, you may work in a dealer workshop, body repair shop, or service and repair center. Experienced auto mechanics can even go on to become independent technicians, offering mobile services to vehicle owners.

With vehicle technologies constantly changing and developing, the auto mechanic industry is changing rapidly, but job prospects are promising for qualified candidates who are willing to keep up with the latest technologies. According to a report by the Bureau of Labor Statistics in April 2018, the demand for auto mechanics was expected to grow 6 percent between 2016 and 2026, which is in line with the average growth rate for most occupations. Most employers require auto mechanics to complete a program at a postsecondary institute, such as a technical college, and obtain industry certification, usually from the National Institute of Automotive Service Excellence (ASE).

If you are someone who likes working with your hands and taking time to figure out what the problem is, and you have technological aptitude and a willingness to keep up with new technology, the field of auto mechanics could be a great career choice for you.

A DAY ON THE JOB

There is really no such thing as a typical day for an auto mechanic, and this aspect is one of the great joys of the job. Depending on where technicians work, they may be rebuilding an engine one moment and changing spark plugs the next. Mechanics may go from repairing a front axle to replacing an air filter. They may work on foreign models or domestic—or both. They may be diagnosing the

The tools that mechanics use vary from day to day, depending on what they're working on. They include old-fashioned hand tools as well as complex diagnostics systems.

problem on an air-cooled 1977 Volkswagen bus one day and repairing the self-parking mechanism on a Lexus LS 460 the next. Everything depends on the kind of mechanic they are, what model cars their shop or dealership specializes in, and what their area of expertise is.

The tools used on the job will vary greatly, from old-fashioned hand tools and grease and oil, to power tools and diagnostic computers. In a large dealership garage or chain service center such as Goodwrench, Midas, or Jiffy Lube, mechanics may start their day by reporting to a service manager, who will decide which of the many vehicles to begin working on. In a smaller shop, the mechanic may chat with the customer to find out what seems to be wrong with the car and then go for a test drive to further diagnose the problem. Then the mechanic would begin working on the car and fixing the problems. The unpredictability of the job, of course, is one of its advantages. It keeps the work interesting and makes every day different from the one before it. It also ensures that the mechanic keeps up to date on the latest models, the newest techniques, and the most reliable repairs.

Skills of the Trade

There are a number of skills that auto mechanics use on a regular basis. If you're wondering whether you're cut out to be an auto mechanic, think about whether you have these essential skills.

- **Detail oriented: Many duties of an auto mechanic require precise and intricate work. Paying careful attention to details can help a mechanic quickly spot the problem with a vehicle, saving both time and money.**
- **Customer service: Customers want to work with a mechanic who makes them feel comfortable and seems trustworthy, so having strong customer service skills goes a long way toward establishing successful business practices.**
- **Communication: The average customer doesn't understand the technical jargon of car mechanics. That's why a successful auto mechanic needs to be able to clearly and effectively communicate the issues in a way that their customers can understand.**

(continued on the next page)

(continued from the previous page)

- **Problem solving: Sometimes a problem with a vehicle is obvious, and sometimes it's very hard to diagnose. A good auto mechanic should be able to think outside the box and be willing to explore possibilities beyond the obvious solution.**
- **Technical aptitude: Cars are becoming more and more complicated, and so is the technology that makes them function. Auto mechanics need to have a strong working knowledge of advanced diagnostics systems and be willing to keep learning to keep up with the latest vehicle technologies.**
- **Physical ability: Auto mechanics often need to be able to fit into tight spaces, do some heavy lifting, climb onto elevated workspaces, or work in tough weather conditions.**
- **Versatility: The work of an auto mechanic can change from day to day. People who are versatile and thrive in a changing work environment are likely well suited to a career as an auto mechanic.**

HIGH SCHOOL CLASSES

Don't sit back and wait for graduation day to begin developing your interest in automotive mechanics. Watch for opportunities all around you, and, when you spot one, grab it. These experiences will either help you decide that mechanics is not the way you want to go, or confirm that you find it fascinating, are good at it, and are eager to learn as much as you can.

If you're interested in becoming an auto mechanic, it's a good idea to take plenty of science classes in school. Mechanics use science in their work every day.

To get a head start in your career, make sure you take the appropriate classes in high school. Which ones are they? Classes in math and English are important, of course, as you will be working with both numbers and words on a daily basis. In addition, a strong background in science, including electronics, computer technology, and physics, is also helpful. Obviously, if your school offers any classes or workshops on car maintenance and repair or small engine work, take those as well. Some high schools also partner with local community colleges to create vocational technical courses. Several times a week, you may travel to the college to take a course that will earn you both high school credit and invaluable hands-on experience.

AFTER HIGH SCHOOL

Once you're done with high school, you will need to get further education and practical training before you start searching for your first job as an auto mechanic. There are a couple of ways to obtain such preparation. You can attend community college classes, usually for a period of six to twelve months, or you can go to a post-secondary (after graduation from high school) vocational school for two years and earn an associate's degree. Both options will offer you a combination of classroom instruction and hands-on experience and practice. They will both have the most up-to-date technical data for teaching, as well as the newest types of diagnostic equipment. An associate's degree program usually combines all of this instruction with additional courses in English, math, and the sciences.

You can find community colleges and vocational schools in your area by searching online. Some of these schools are statewide or even nationwide institutions, with local campuses near you. The Universal Technical Institute, for example, has campuses in Arizona, Pennsylvania, Texas, Florida, and elsewhere. Some websites, such as MechanicSchools.com, provide information regarding vocational schools throughout the nation. Bear in mind that technical and vocational colleges are great, but they also can cost a lot of money. Junior colleges are a terrific alternative and they are usually much less expensive.

Some auto manufacturers and dealers offer their own two-year associate's degree programs. Once enrolled, students alternate between working in the dealer's service department and going to school every six to twelve weeks.

NATIONAL INSTITUTE FOR AUTOMOTIVE SERVICE EXCELLENCE (ASE)

In the late 1960s, the automotive repair industry was under intense scrutiny. Countless complaints of fraud had been forwarded to the US Congress, and the government was finally taking action. During the hearings, it was determined that the real problem was not mechanics trying to swindle customers, but mechanics who were simply not adequately trained for the job. Since there was no official way to identify and distinguish between the skilled technicians and the poorly trained ones through professional licensing or certification, customers often made the wrong choices when choosing a mechanic. Anyone with a toolbox could put out a sign saying he or she was a mechanic, but which ones could really be trusted?

Congress decided the solution was to pass a number of laws and regulations regarding the licensing of technicians. Those in the business, however, were not so sure this action was the best option. Instead, the National Automobile Dealers Association and the former Motor Vehicle Manufacturers Association banded together to create the ASE. The ASE remains the primary certification institute for auto mechanics in the United States and sets the basic standards for the industry.

The ASE is the main certification institution for auto mechanics in the United States. Technicians will have a much easier time finding a job once they are ASE certified.

ASE CERTIFICATION EXAMS

The ASE has a set of tests that mechanics can take to get certification to prove that they are thoroughly knowledgeable in their area or areas of specialization. This certification helps customers to distinguish the competent from the incompetent technicians by setting a basic standard. The ASE series of Automobile and Light Truck Certification Tests (A series) includes tests in the following nine primary categories of maintenance and repair:

- Engine repair
- Automatic transmission/transaxle
- Manual drive train and axles
- Suspension and steering
- Brakes
- Electrical/electronic systems
- Heating and air-conditioning
- Engine performance
- Light vehicle diesel engines

Each test has between forty and eighty multiple-choice questions, many of them accompanied by detailed schematics and illustrations. When technicians pass one exam, they receive a certificate and a patch denoting expertise in that skill area. Technicians who pass eight out of these nine tests (the light vehicle diesel engines test is not required) are certified as "master technicians." Before each test can be taken, a technician must have worked in the field for two years, or one year plus attendance at an accredited training program. A number of preparation guides for these tests can be found in book form, as well as on the ASE website.

To maintain certification, tests have to be retaken every five years. This way, the technician stays up to date on all of the changing technology that is part of the profession. These recertification tests are about half as long as the original ones. The ASE offers additional series of tests in the following specializations:

- Advanced engine performance specialist
- Alternate fuels
- Auto maintenance and light repair

- Automobile service consultant
- Collision repair and refinish
- Damage analysis and estimating
- Electronic diesel engine diagnosis
- Engine machinist
- Light duty hybrid/electric vehicle specialist
- Medium/heavy truck
- School bus
- Transit bus
- Truck equipment
- Parts specialist
- Undercar specialist

Auto mechanics are are not required by law to take these tests, but most employers require them. Those with ASE certification are more likely to get hired, especially by the larger garages and dealerships. Those with ASE certification are also likely to get paid more. Having the ASE patches and certification will make someone a more valued employee, a more skilled mechanic, and a more trusted personal service technician.

ADAPTING TO NEW TECHNOLOGIES

"Having the skills and ability to utilize today's technology in automotive repair is crucial for anyone entering into this field," said Art Jacobsen, former vice president of CarMD, in an interview with Tamra Orr. "Vehicles are highly computerized, and being comfortable working with computers and scanning tools is a must for anyone entering this field. Service information, for the most part, is now all computerized. This is not a 'learn this instead of that' kind of proposal. This is now the minimum you need to enter this industry. These skills must be strong and combined with automotive-specific knowledge. The two areas need to work together to determine the root cause of what is wrong with a vehicle."

Bearing these facts in mind, it's a good idea for prospective auto mechanics to keep their backgrounds well rounded. In addition to needing automotive skills, they should also be able to approach problems in a logical and systematic way, and be highly adept at using complicated computer programming systems. Jacobsen added, "Being well-read and understanding new technologies and how they are applied and developed for today's vehicles are essential. Anybody going into automotive repair should be familiar with the government regulations."

Chapter 2

SERVICE AND DIAGNOSTIC TECHNICIANS

Many auto mechanics work as service technicians or diagnostic technicians, also known as drivability technicians. Service technicians do routine servicing on cars and vans, checking the oil and fluid levels and replacing them if recommended by manufacturers' guidelines. They check to make sure the fuel and ignition systems are operating reliably and efficiently. Service technicians also make sure the major electrical and mechanical parts of the vehicle are functioning properly. They diagnose problems like poor starting or excessive fuel consumption. Several of these duties overlap with the work of a diagnostic technician.

Diagnostic or drivability technicians utilize special tools to diagnose problems in the vehicle's electrical

There are so many things that can go wrong with a vehicle. Mechanics use special diagnostic tools to figure out what the problem is when a car is not running smoothly.

ignition, emissions, and engine management systems. As automotive systems become more complex, diagnostic technicians have an increasingly important role to play in the workshop.

Most service technicians and diagnostic technicians work in car repair shops. More experienced mechanics may work independently and offer a mobile service to customers.

DIAGNOSING AND FIXING THE PROBLEM

Diagnosing what is wrong with a vehicle is often tricky, just like determining what is wrong when a person is ill. There are so many auto parts that can malfunction that it can be challenging to figure out which one is performing badly and why. It frequently takes a combination of years of practical experience, old-fashioned "elbow grease" working with hand tools, computerized diagnostics, and a sharp set of eyes and ears to figure it all out.

Although mechanics may get some valuable information from customers, more often than not they tend to describe problems in vague terms, like "sputter," "ping," or "buzz." These kinds of descriptions rarely pinpoint a problem, but they may still provide a few clues. So it's important to listen to customers, even if their mechanical knowledge is lacking.

Once the diagnosis has been made on a car, it's time to decide what to do about it. Again, effective auto repair requires years of practical experience and mechanical knowledge to determine not only what to fix or replace, but also how to go about doing it properly. If new parts are needed, the technician will often have to contact a variety of parts suppliers to find the right part for the right price. The cost of parts is added to the expected cost of the labor (usually a per-hour charge), and that price is given to the customer for approval. This price is known as an estimate. If the customer agrees to the proposed price of the repair, work can begin.

Of course, not all the work that mechanics do is repairs. Many technicians spend their days performing routine maintenance and inspections. They typically follow a checklist of what to examine, such as belts, hoses, plugs, brakes, the fuel and exhaust systems, and tires.

The Most Common Car Troubles

There are countless things that can go wrong with an automobile, but some are far more common than others. Some car parts wear out faster because they get more use. Here are the ten areas that car service technicians must repair the most often:

- **Brake system**
- **Engine lubrication (oil changes) and air filters**
- **Radiator**
- **Ignition or electronic control**
- **Steering/suspension**
- **Carburetor/fuel system**
- **Electrical system**
- **Transmission/clutch/rear axle**
- **Climate control (air-conditioning, heating, and defrosting)**
- **Exhaust system**

This step helps prevent major breakdowns and repairs "down the road."

Once the work on a car is finished, technicians may take the vehicle for a test drive and then let the customer know that the job is done. The work usually does not stop there, however. Now it's time for cleaning the bay and tools and getting ready for the next car in line outside the garage.

Being a service technician can be a fascinating job. It constantly changes with the times and with each technological advance. New skills must always be acquired and new mechanical challenges met with each new model of car that rolls off the assembly line. Auto repair and maintenance is work that people will always need, no matter the direction technology may take.

MICHELE WINN, MASTER TROUBLESHOOTER

Michele Winn, lead diagnostic technician at Beck Service Center in Indianapolis, Indiana, decided to become an auto mechanic while she was working in the office of an auto repair shop. Realizing she wanted to learn more about the technical aspects of the work, Winn enrolled in the fifteen-month Automotive Service Management Associate Degree program at Lincoln Technical Institute, where she graduated with a 4.0 grade point average and perfect attendance.

Winn went on to work for Linder Technical Services in Indianapolis, troubleshooting problem vehicles referred from other shops and teaching ongoing education classes for auto mechanics. She enjoys the challenge of working

A vehicle's engine is made up of many complex components, including an alternator. The alternator generates power for the vehicle's electrical systems.

with different vehicles and learning new skills, though she admits it's hard work.

"Every day is different. I work on different vehicles with different types of problems all the time. Plus, the technology that goes into new vehicles is changing at a very rapid rate, so I am always learning about new designs, parts, and ways to service new vehicles," Winn said in an interview with Automotive Schools.

She went on to say that one of the biggest challenges of the job is keeping up with changing technology:

> Just like a doctor would attend a clinic to learn about new procedures, we constantly need to update ourselves on the latest technology on today's vehicles. In my opinion, doctors have it easy. The human body really only comes in two models, male and female. In the case of vehicles, there are new model vehicles introduced every year along with all the changes in computer systems and electronics that are on the existing models. We have to keep in touch with all of it.

GETTING A HEAD START

Even though you may still be a student in high school, you do not have to wait to get started in the field of automotive service. There are a number of steps you can take right now that will give you a head start later on when you either pursue further education or begin looking for a job.

To get started, treat your interest in automotive care as a homework assignment or research paper and start studying the field. There are several things you can do

Many service technicians work at auto repair shops. The work here varies from day to day, based on the needs of the customers who bring their vehicles in for maintenance and repair.

to begin familiarizing yourself with the auto care industry and the necessary educational preparation. Search the internet to see what you can find out about educational programs, standard certification tests, and potential internships. There are hundreds of sites to explore on the topic. Stop by both school and public libraries to see what books and other resource materials they have to offer. They frequently have automotive how-to books and videos available to loan.

If there is a local car garage that has caught your eye, go in and see if you can chat with the owner for a few minutes about the business. Stop by a dealership that sells your favorite brand of car and ask if you can interview a couple of the mechanics. Be prepared for them to say yes and have your questions written out and ready to go, just in case. These people are busy workers, and you don't want to take up too much of their time.

Ask your guidance counselor about any internships or apprenticeships that may be available in the area. Explore the vocational schools and community colleges in your region. What courses, certification, and degree programs do they offer? What are the academic requirements, course times, and cost?

Read the local ads in the newspaper and see if any garages or instructors are offering noncredit community courses in mechanics. Can you take some of these classes now while you are still in high school? Keep an eye out for ads and opportunities that are not necessarily focused exclusively on cars but on small engines, too, such as a class in repairing lawn mowers or garden tractors. Perhaps someone is offering a weekend class on fixing boat engines or motorcycle maintenance. Seize as many of these opportunities as possible. They might help you refine your interests as you develop solid overall mechanical skills.

Let your parents and neighbors know about your interest as well. They might know someone who can help you or at least invite you over to watch them replace a set of spark plugs or a clutch cable. Check out the bulletin boards in grocery stores, libraries, your school, city hall, and other public gathering spots. These places are often where listings for small automotive and mechanics classes will be posted. If you're especially interested in a certain type of class but can't find one, why not take the time to write up what you're looking for and post it on the same bulletin boards or in an online forum? You might find enough like-minded people to start a class, or at least an instructor who is willing to teach you the basics.

Chapter 3

SPECIALIZED MECHANICS

Many larger workshops employ auto mechanics who specialize in specific areas, such as those with expert knowledge of auto air-conditioning units, auto brake systems, and transmission systems, and those who specialize in front-end auto mechanics. If you decide you're particularly interested in one or more of these areas of auto mechanics, you may decide to get specialized training.

AIR-CONDITIONING TECHNICIANS

Some auto mechanics specialize in working with automotive air-conditioning systems. This job includes installing and repairing air conditioners and their components, including

The air-conditioning system in a vehicle is complicated. Some auto mechanics specialize in working with these units, and the ASE offers a certification test on vehicle heating and air-conditioning systems.

compressors, condensers, and controls. These technicians must be specially trained to handle refrigerants—the fluids used in air-conditioning systems.

Mechanics interested in specializing in air-conditioning systems can get qualified for this position by taking the ASE test on heating and air conditioning, which is part of the ASE Certification Test Series for Automobile and Light Truck Certification.

BRAKE AND TRANSMISSION TECHNICIANS

Brake technicians diagnose problems with the vehicle's braking system, adjust the brakes, replace the brakes' rotors and pads when necessary, and repair other components of the brake system. This work helps to ensure vehicle safety. Transmission technicians focus on the power train and steering components, including gears, couplings, and hydraulic pumps. These specialists must have extensive knowledge of the electronics systems that control the transmission system, and they must be able to diagnose electrical and hydraulic problems.

Mechanics can become qualified to work with brake and transmission systems by taking the ASE tests on brakes, automatic transmission/transaxle, or manual drive train and axels. All these tests are offered as part of the ASE Certification Test Series for Automobile and Light Truck Certification.

FRONT-END TECHNICIANS

Front-end technicians focus on diagnosing problems with the front-end assembly of the vehicle, which includes the steering and the suspension. The steering and suspension impact the way the vehicle handles the road. Diagnosing problems with the front-end assembly may include inspecting tires for wear and damage, as well as inspecting and replacing other parts of the vehicle's front end.

Mechanics who choose to specialize in front-end work can get qualified by taking the ASE test on steering and suspension, which is one of the tests included in the ASE Certification Test Series for Automobile and Light Truck Certification.

BECOMING A SPECIALIST

Some doctors, rather than becoming general practitioners, decide to become specialists in the care of a specific part of the body. In the same way, mechanics can choose to maintain and repair a range of vehicles and makes

Different types of vehicles require different care. Some mechanics choose to specialize in working with a specific type of vehicle, such as all-terrain vehicles (ATVs).

and models, or they can choose a specialty. It might be only one model of car. It might be only one particular system, such as the exhaust system or transmission. A mechanic might only work on scooters, speedboats, high-performance cars, or all-terrain vehicles (ATVs). Some technicians might devote themselves to a specific make of foreign car. Others may specialize in maintaining a city's fleet of buses, subways, or streetcars.

Areas of specialization can get incredibly specific. For example, there are a handful of experts on the maintenance and repair of air-cooled Volkswagen buses. That area is all they work on. Becoming an invaluable specialist or an equally expert generalist—a highly skilled, all-around mechanic—all depends on what interests you like the most and what jobs you can find in your area. Some areas of specialization are more lucrative than others. Mechanics who specialize in working with electric and hybrid vehicles are becoming increasingly in demand.

Taking the time to read through the nine different examinations given by the ASE might help you determine if you want to specialize in a specific area of vehicle repair and maintenance. Read the questions and study the different divisions within each section. Which appeals to you the most?

THE IMPORTANCE OF BEING WELL ROUNDED

Even if a specific make and model or automotive system appeals to you and you think you might want to specialize in it, it is always wise to develop a broad range of mechanical skills to boost your employability. Tony Molla, vice president of communications for the National Institute for Automotive Service Excellence, told Josh Green of MyNC.com how many opportunities there are for good, well-rounded auto technicians:

> Having technical skills can open up quite a few possibilities for those in the automotive industry, but even other industries like aerospace recognize the value of an applicant with a technical background. Many parts manufacturers, for example, love to have regional sales representatives with technical backgrounds, since such an individual would not only understand the products and how they are used, they also understand the customer very well. Having a good mastery of electronics, knowing how to use sophisticated test equipment, and being proficient with the use of tools can qualify an individual for a great many things, from shop management to customer service positions. The most obvious opportunities for technicians right now are in the heavy-duty segment, and most of these companies will provide the ongoing training a technician needs to keep their skills sharp and cope with advancing automotive technology.

THE RIGHT TOOLS FOR THE JOB

Having great dexterity—being "good with your hands"—is an important quality for anyone going into mechanics. Equally important is having the proper hand tools for the profession. The availability and quality of tools are often the main keys to whether a job is slow and frustrating or smooth and efficient.

Tools are certainly one of a mechanic's most essential helpers and greatest investments. Most technicians have a personal set of tools that they have collected over the years. In addition, workplaces supply some of the biggest, most complex, and expensive types of equipment such as diagnostic computers, pneumatic drills, hydraulic lifts, and other large power tools.

Tools of the Trade

What tools do mechanics use most frequently? In any given day, a mechanic will use enough different hand tools to fill a large toolbox. You should start with the basics, including the following tools and equipment:

- **Drain pan**
- **Gloves**
- **Rags**
- **Safety glasses**
- **Earplugs**
- **Funnels**
- **Screwdrivers**
- **Wrenches**
- **Hammers**
- **Pliers**
- **Socket sets**
- **Allen keys**
- **Wire cutters**
- **Pry bars**
- **Wire brushes**
- **Feeler gauges**
- **Calipers**

Power tools are also essential to a mechanic's daily work. An electric motor, a compressed air motor, or a gasoline engine powers them. The tools can either be portable (handheld) or stationary. They are typically used for cutting, shaping, drilling, sanding, painting, grinding, and polishing. Some power tools that you might use in automotive work and would probably be provided by your employer include:

- **Drill presses**
- **Bench grinders**
- **Lathes**
- **Pneumatic wenches**
- **Air compressors**
- **Compression gauges**
- **Welders/flame-cutting equipment**
- **Jacks**
- **Hoists**

Auto mechanics need to know how to use a wide range of tools, including power tools such as bench grinders. These tools are likely to be provided by employers.

Besides these hand and power tools, you will probably use computerized diagnostic equipment that remains at the dealership or garage where you work. Today, vehicles that come into a repair shop are often linked up to computers that test their various systems. A readout compares the test results with a set of benchmark standards issued by the manufacturer. The technician watches for any deviations from the norm. Dealerships and garages get regular updates from car manufacturers about specific car models, their systems, and individual parts to add to their on-site library of technical manuals. They also have access to technical service bulletins and internet databases. These sources of information provide new technical details, highlight common problems, and explain new maintenance procedures and repair techniques. Computers also help diagnose problems with the high-tech equipment installed in most modern cars, such as global positioning systems (GPS) and self-parking mechanisms.

THE EVOLUTION OF CARS, TECHNICIANS, AND THEIR TOOLS

Cars and other vehicles are far more complicated than they used to be, and so are the tools that are needed to check and repair them. Mechanical systems have been more or less replaced by onboard computer systems, so it's essential that the technicians of the future are adept at using these computer-controlled systems and computerized scan tools to diagnose the problem. Says Art Jacobsen:

> Vehicles, for the most part, still combine gasoline with oxygen and use combustion to generate power. The change is the integration of the computer and ALL of its computing power to control how the vehicle operates. It is often said that the computers in today's vehicles are more complex than the computers from the Apollo missions. The trick is being able to get the diagnostic information from the vehicle computer, determine the root cause of the failure, and repair it.

Chapter 4

AUTO BODY REPAIR TECHNICIANS

Some auto mechanics decide to focus on the body of the vehicle, rather than the engine. The work of a body repair technician includes replacing damaged or worn body parts, like panels, fenders, or headlights. Sometimes parts of the vehicle need to be repaired because of an accident, and sometimes it's just due to everyday usage. In cases where there is a lot of damage to a specific component, the auto repair technician needs to decide whether it makes more sense economically to fix it or replace it. Sometimes these technicians do cosmetic repairs in cases where a vehicle has been scratched or dented.

Car accidents happen every day. Auto repair technicians work on vehicles that have been in collisions to repair the body of the car and give it a fresh new look.

Body repair technicians may specialize in refinishing vehicles. This area can involve working in a spray booth, repairing damage or giving an old car a fresh new look. Vehicle refinishers can also help customers personalize their vehicles using special finishing techniques and materials.

AUTO BODY REPAIR

Every single day there are thousands of traffic accidents. Although that is not a happy fact, it is what keeps auto body shops in business. If you decide to specialize as an automotive body worker, it will be your job to remove or repair dents, replace damaged parts, and straighten out bent frames and structures.

To do these jobs, you will most likely use equipment like alignment machines powered by hydraulic pressure. They will help you get broken parts back into alignment. Specific benchmark standards will guide you in figuring out where each piece has to go to work properly again. A pneumatic metal-cutting gun may be used to repair body panels, and dents are fixed through a combination of pneumatic hammers, hand prying bars, and hydraulic jacks. Pick hammers and punches can be used to take out the smallest pits. Plastic panels will need to be molded back into place through the use of a hot-air welding gun or simply hot water and lots of patience.

Along with a background in general auto repair, an automotive body worker should be excellent at reading technical manuals and diagrams, as well as measuring and doing quick mathematical figuring. The ASE offers certification in collision repair through four of its exams.

Inside the ASE Test for Painting and Refinishing

What kind of knowledge and expertise is required to become an auto body technician or vehicle refinisher? Here are a few sample multiple-choice questions taken from the official 2017 ASE study guide for the collision repair and refinish tests.

1. **Before applying paint, a painter should select the fluid nozzle and needle based on the:**
   a. size of the job
   b. type of coating
   c. spray booth manufacturer
   d. painter preference
   (answer: type of coating)

2. **When closing a convertible top, the driver's side has a larger gap than the passenger's side before locking in place. Which of these could be the cause?**
   a. bent roof frame
   b. shrunken convertible top material
   c. normal condition
   d. bent B-pillar
   (answer: bent roof frame)

3. **Which type of damage is LEAST likely to occur on a unibody vehicle?**
   a. sidesway
   b. diamond
   c. sag
   d. twist
   (answer: diamond)

CAREER ADVICE FROM AN AUTO BODY TECHNICIAN

In an interview for Dr. Kit Career Videos, Leslie, an auto body technician at Bay Chevrolet, describes a typical day at work and discusses what he likes and dislikes about his job. In this line of work you've got to be prepared to get dirty and to work outdoors in all weather conditions, Leslie says, but despite all that, he finds his work very rewarding. "If you can take a car that's damaged and put it back like it was when it was new, it's amazing."

Leslie advises teens who may be interested in auto body repair work to take high school classes in math, technology, and even art to prepare for a career in the field. "If you're interested in this kind of work and you're still in high school, my advice to you would be to work on your own car. You can start off by removing dents, scratches, and occasionally a fender too here and there. That's how I learned."

AUTO GLASS REPAIR

Some automotive technicians choose to specialize in glass repair and replacement. Car windows and windshields get cracked and broken all the time through accidents and collisions. Auto glass repair technicians check window and windshield damage to determine whether it's a chip or crack that can be fixed, or whether the whole window or windshield needs to be replaced. These specialists have to make sure the windshield frame is clean and hasn't rusted before applying sealant when inserting new glass. Other responsibilities include removing molding, removing pieces of broken glass, applying primer to metal, and testing for leaks and noise.

Auto glass repair is a specialization within the field of auto mechanics. If you're interested in working with glass, there are a number of training programs where you can learn this skill.

Many collision repair certificate programs at community or vocational schools offer a course in auto glass service and repair. Organizations such as the National Windshield Repair Association (NWRA), the National Glass Association (NGA), and the Independent Glass Association (IGA) also offer their own certifications for auto glass repair technicians. Though these certifications are not required by law, many employers look for them. Training for those interested in earning their certification is provided by a number of different organizations, including the NGA, Auto Glass Academy, and Automotive Glass Consultants.

Get Your Nails Done While You Wait for an Oil Change!

Patrice Banks used to dread taking her car to get the oil changed. "I was tired of feeling helpless and having to go talk to a guy," she told NPR's Terri Gross. Banks wanted to find a female auto mechanic to go to, but she couldn't. Although women make up more than half of the drivers in the United States, less than 2 percent of mechanics are women, according to *NBC Nightly News*. Banks decided to take matters into her own hands by going back to school to become a mechanic.

In 2016, Banks opened her own car service center, Girls Auto Clinic repair center in Upper Derby, Pennsylvania, which caters to female customers and is staffed by all female mechanics. "It's no secret most women hate their automotive buying and repair experiences because we feel misunderstood, taken advantage of, and/or mistreated," reads the clinic's website. Girls Auto Clinic aims to address this situation by providing a car service experience that is "based on trust, education, inclusion, and empowerment."

Girls Auto Clinic even has a nail and blowout salon next door! "'[For] women, it's like a chore, we hate going in to get our oil changed ... But we look forward to doing things like getting our nails done. And so I thought it would just be cute and just [be] the cherry on the top when I tell people, 'I have a shop that caters to women. Full service auto repair, all female mechanics!' They're like, 'Woah!'

(continued on the next page)

(continued from the previous page)

I'm like, 'And there's a nail salon there.'" Banks is also the author of *Girls Auto Clinic Glove Box Guide*, in which she tells her story and provides car maintenance tips.

LIFELONG LEARNING ON THE JOB

Once you have completed your education and find your first job, don't think you are finished learning. The automotive industry is constantly changing, and its vehicles are always becoming more complex and high-tech. For this reason, continuing education is absolutely necessary for the technician who wishes to remain knowledgeable and skilled. Employers typically send their technicians to manufacturers' training centers to learn how to repair new model cars or get specific training on repairing individual components. Other times, factory representatives will come to the dealership to present workshops to the technicians.

Experts in the field state that it takes two to five years on the job before veteran mechanics consider newer employees to be fully qualified service technicians. It requires one to two additional years to become familiar with every type of car repair. Moreover, if you specialize in one particular area, such as auto body repair, that can take an additional one to two years to truly master.

When it comes to automotive maintenance and repair, it's important to remember that practice makes perfect.

Being an auto mechanic is a highly skilled profession. It takes years of experience to become proficient. Even once you get your first job, it's important to keep learning and developing your skills.

It takes time to develop talent and to gain knowledge and experience to become a truly competent and skilled technician. You won't learn these skills quickly, but with time, you can become a valued and respected employee who makes cars far safer and more reliable.

Chapter 5

BUSES, MOTORCYCLES, AND MORE

Cars are not the only vehicles that auto mechanics may choose to work on. You could decide you want to pursue a career in working with larger trucks and buses, farm equipment, construction vehicles, motorcycles, or any number of other vehicles with large or small engines. Diesel mechanics (technicians who work on buses, large trucks, and other vehicles with diesel engines), small engine mechanics, and heavy vehicle mechanics require specialized training for these specialized professions.

According to 2018 data from the Bureau of Labor Statistics, jobs for diesel mechanics, small engine mechanics, and heavy vehicle mechanics were projected to grow at the respective rates of 9 percent, 5 percent, and 8 percent between 2016 and 2026—average growth rates that are similar to the 6 percent growth rate projected for general auto mechanics. Mechanics in these fields are generally required to have postsecondary training at a technical institute and industry certification. In addition, the ASE offers certification tests in a wide variety of areas, including specialized tests for those looking to work with diesel engines, buses, and medium or heavy trucks.

BIGGER VEHICLES, BIGGER ENGINES

If you enjoy working with the bigger, more powerful machines, a career maintaining and repairing heavy vehicles and mobile equipment may be a perfect choice for you. These are the vehicles that are used in construction, agriculture, heavy industry, freight and shipping, and railroads. Technicians repair, replace, clean, lubricate, and maintain heavy equipment. This equipment can include tractors, buses, combines, road graders, cranes, bulldozers, and rail cars. Because many of these machines use hydraulics, technicians must learn how to deal with fluid leaks, ruptured hoses, and worn-out gaskets. Many of the engines used in such large equipment, as well as in trucks, trains, and buses, are diesel engines. Working on them requires specialized training in working with diesel fuels. Some employees send experienced technicians to training classes led by manufacturers to learn about the latest diesel technology.

THE ART OF MOTORCYCLE MAINTENANCE

Another angle to pursue within mechanics is working with two-wheeled and three-wheeled vehicles. There are millions of motorcycles, scooters, mopeds, dirt bikes, and ATVs on the road that need regular maintenance and repair.

Working with large vehicles such as tractors and heavy trucks requires a different skill set from regular auto mechanics, so it's necessary to get specialized training.

Some bike mechanics work in garages, while a number of them work for specific dealerships, such as Harley-Davidson, Honda, Yamaha, Suzuki, or Kawasaki.

Classes in motorcycle mechanics include information on repairing forks, transmissions, and drive chains. Students learn how to dismantle engines and replace parts like magnetos, carburetors, and generators. They practice removing cylinder heads and grind valves and hammering out dents and bends, as well as welding tears and breaks. Manual dexterity is extremely important for motorcycle mechanics because the areas they work within are much smaller and closer together than what is under the hood of a car.

High-Performance Cars

High-performance cars have a great deal of power relative to their overall weight. Sometimes they are thought to be the same as sports cars, but there are subtle differences. High-performance cars have extremely powerful engines

Many people think that high-performance cars are the same as race cars, but there are some differences. For a start, high-performance cars are designed for the racetrack, not the road.

(continued on the next page)

(continued from the previous page)

and are designed not for the road but for the racetrack. They can go extremely fast without losing control. Because of this feature, their structure and engines are often somewhat different from those of the typical passenger car. This distinction means specialized mechanics are needed to work on them.

High-performance car specialists require specific training to make sure the vehicle is reliable even when placed under severe stress. To do so, they frequently use engine analyzers, handheld scanners, and computerized diagnostic equipment. Not only do these technicians need to understand every aspect of the vehicles they are working on, but they also have to learn the tricks to getting every ounce of performance out of the race cars. The drivers' livelihoods—and lives—depend on it.

FURTHER AFIELD

The same skills and interests that brought you to the field of mechanics can take you in several other exciting directions as well. Some possibilities include marine mechanics, avionics, and small-engine repair. Working on these nonautomotive vehicles can be both fascinating and lucrative. The work can take you to interesting places, like marinas, aircraft carriers, and rocket launchpads. Furthermore, because these machines are often so crucial to commerce and defense, the pay is great.

OUT ON THE WATER

There are more than 12.8 million recreational boats cruising the waters of the country's lakes, rivers, and oceans. Marine or motorboat mechanics are needed to maintain and service all of them. Inboard motors are usually found on large boats like cabin cruisers, cargo ships, ferries, oil tankers, submarines, and commercial fishing boats.

Because boats are so big, repairs are typically performed by trained mechanics who go to the docks, shipyards, and marinas to work on them. Outboard engines, on the other hand, are typically found on small boats, Jet Skis, yachts, and other motorized watercraft. Repairs on these lighter craft are done in garages because the smaller engines can be brought in and left behind. Technicians work not only on engines, but also on propellers, plumbing, and steering mechanisms. On larger ships, they may also work on air-conditioning and refrigeration systems. Common maintenance procedures include checking parts for safety; replacing wiring; inspecting pumps, gears, and rings; and realigning the steering.

Depending on where you live, repair and maintenance of marine craft can be seasonal work, so it may be difficult to find enough to do during the fall and winter months. Living near resort areas or coastal regions, where the weather allows for boating year-round, can be the best choice. You may work directly for a marina or for a dealership or boat manufacturer. No matter where you work, you will most likely spend a great deal of time out in the sun and near the water—a great job perk.

Marine mechanics can go to professional technical schools to learn the business and enter two-year programs to earn an associate's degree.

UP IN THE AIR

Another type of specialization you might want to explore is avionics, or aircraft mechanics. Avionics programs certified by the Federal Aviation Administration (FAA) are offered by schools across the country. These programs range in length from eighteen months to four years.

The field of avionics includes everything from propeller-driven and jet engine commercial passenger planes to helicopters, fighters, and bombers. Aircraft mechanics do a variety of jobs. These include inspecting, maintaining, and repairing aircraft engines, landing gear, instruments, pressurized sections, accessory brakes, valves, pumps, and air-conditioning systems. They check for cracks in the engine, fuselage, wings, and tail using X-rays and magnetic inspection.

Like any qualified mechanic, avionics technicians repair and replace worn or defective parts. They measure tension on the aircraft's control cables. They work on the craft's hydraulics and electrical systems. Avionics technicians work on virtually anything that is involved in both navigation and communication on aircraft, including the weather radar systems. In addition, these mechanics also keep very detailed maintenance records.

SMALL BUT POWERFUL

Another common type of mechanics that you can get involved in is working with small engines. Technicians are

When a lawn mower stops functioning, a mechanic is often needed to get it up and running again. Some mechanics choose to focus on machines with small engines.

needed to repair and service power equipment like chain saws, edge trimmers, lawn mowers, go-carts, portable generators, snowblowers, and snowmobiles. Typically, a technician specializes in a particular type of equipment.

Technicians who choose this field learn how to do everything from replacing a single part to performing a complete overhaul of the equipment. In the case of a ride-on lawn mower or go-cart, they may inspect and clean the engine, brakes, fuel injection systems, plugs, and carburetors, following a set checklist of what needs to be examined. Other times, they perform regular maintenance service to ensure that the machine is working at peak performance. Although most mechanics rely on hand tools for this job, some may also use more complex tools. These can include compression gauges, ammeters, voltmeters, and computerized engine analyzers.

SOMETHING FOR EVERYONE

With the immense diversity found in the world of automotive technology, there truly is something for everyone. Whether you want to focus on vehicles small or large, vintage or new, American or foreign, transmissions or auto body, general or specialized, ample opportunities are there for you. Chances are, a job opening is as close as your local classified ads.

Chapter 6

ADAPTING TO A CHANGING INDUSTRY

As auto technology changes, so does the work of auto mechanics. In fact, there are not many industries that are changing as rapidly as the auto industry. The environmental need to explore alternative fuels combined with advances in auto technology means that there are more and more hybrid cars and electric vehicles (EVs) on the road. Meanwhile, the technology of autonomous, or "self-driving," cars is developing at a rapid rate. It's vital for those who are interested in pursuing a career in auto mechanics to be prepared for these changes.

That said, for those who are committed to keeping up with a changing industry, the future looks promising. The Bureau of Labor Statistics projected in April 2018 that the auto industry would need almost forty-six thousand new technicians between 2016 and 2026, but the number of students going into the industry is dropping. In fact, there is such a shortage of qualified mechanics that car dealerships and auto manufacturers are now creating their own recruiting programs and visiting trade fairs and technical schools to recruit young mechanics. According

Autonomous, or "self-driving," cars are changing the world of auto mechanics. Technicians of the future need to learn to adapt to new technology to thrive in the profession.

to Norman Meyersohn in a 2017 *New York Times* article, "to replenish the entry-level ranks as technicians change jobs or retire, automakers need to start at a more basic skill level, expanding the range of their own programs and partnering with private technical schools to reverse the technician deficit." So, for young people looking to get into auto mechanics, it's a great time to be starting a career in the industry.

AN ONBOARD TECHNICIAN

As vehicles have become more technologically advanced and computerized, manufacturers have installed a number of computerized self-checks within each model. Most new cars now feature monitors that constantly check systems for proper operation. Some of these monitors are continuous, meaning they run whenever the engine is running. Some of them are discontinuous, meaning they run through their internal checklists only once per trip.

A number of products also exist to help the owner keep a close eye on how his or her car, van, SUV, or other vehicle is operating. One of the most popular ones is CarMD. It was developed to help drivers know if something is wrong and what to do about it. "CarMD works by tapping into your vehicle's onboard computer system and extracting information about the current operating condition of your vehicle," explains Art Jacobsen. "This information is then cross-referenced with CarMD's massive online database that is built with repair information from ASE master technicians nationwide. Our database contains real-world solutions to your vehicle's problems."

CarMD allows the driver to take more responsibility for the care and maintenance of his or her vehicle by consulting online with tens of thousands of technicians. It then provides repair suggestions to try at home or to pass along to a local mechanic.

Just as the best surgeon cannot do the job properly without the right scalpel, monitors, and other instruments, neither can the best automotive technician repair any vehicle without specific tools. Knowing what tools are needed for a given job and how to use them is part of what makes mechanics worth their weight in nuts and bolts!

Filling up on French Fries

One of the most common terms thrown around about vehicles today is "alternative fuels." What exactly qualifies as an alternative fuel? Technically, it is any fuel that is not made from petroleum. Such fuels include the following:

- **Biodiesel (from plant oil or animal fat)**
- **Alcohols (ethanol and methanol)**
- **Electricity (batteries)**
- **Hydrogen**
- **Natural gas**
- **Propane (liquified petroleum gas)**

Ethanol, often known as grain alcohol, is usually made from corn, but sometimes other organic material like rice straw is used. Methanol, known as wood alcohol, is made from coal. It has been used in race cars for decades because

Some cars run on biodiesel fuel made from cooking oil used in restaurants. It may sound funny, but this is one way to avoid harming the environment.

it is safer than gasoline in case of accidental fire. Flexible-fuel vehicles have also been developed for consumers. They operate on alcohol, gasoline, or a combination of the two.

Biodiesel fuels, or those made from vegetable oil or animal fat, are slowly developing into a real energy alternative. They are less harmful to the environment and are fairly easy to come by. Some of the most popular types of biodiesel fuel come from either soybeans or used cooking oil from restaurants. Because this type of fuel is made from plants and animals, it is considered renewable—a definite plus when it comes to often scarce and dwindling energy sources.

The technicians who work on engines powered by one of these alternative fuels must have up-to-date information to maintain and repair them.

ADAPTING TO ALTERNATIVE FUEL ENGINES

Oil supplies are limited and dwindling, and the burning of fossil fuels contributes to global warming and climate change. For this reason, engineers have been trying to create vehicles that are powered by alternative sources of energy. They have come up with several possibilities.

The engine of a hybrid car is powered by both gasoline and electricity. Usually, these cars have gasoline engines but rely on an electric motor when speeding up or climbing

Electric vehicles run on batteries instead of gasoline. This means they have to be plugged in regularly to recharge their batteries and keep going.

hills. The motor includes batteries that are continually recharged while you drive. These cars typically get far better gas mileage than regular cars, sometimes getting as much as 68 miles per gallon (29 kilometers per liter). Examples of hybrids include the Honda Insight, the Hyundai Ioniq, and the Toyota Prius.

Other alternative fuel vehicles are electric vehicles, or EVs. They don't burn gasoline, but they depend on twelve or twenty-four batteries for power. These batteries have to be plugged in each day to recharge. They are designed to go about 200 miles (322 km) between recharging.

Another possibility is the zero-emission vehicle, or ZEV. Like spacecraft, these cars feature fuel cells that are powered with pure hydrogen. The fuel cells convert the hydrogen and oxygen into electricity, which, in turn, powers an electric motor.

As vehicles change, so must the automotive technician's skills and knowledge. When vehicle engines make a shift to electricity, hydrogen, or some other new fuel source, the technician will have to adapt to these new technologies as well. It is one of the challenges that make the job so interesting and cutting edge.

A WHOLE NEW ERA FOR AUTO MECHANICS

Joe Sevart of Kansas City, Missouri, began working in his father's auto service shop at the age of fourteen and is now the owner of the business. In a 2016 interview with Adrienne Green in *The Atlantic*, he talked about the changes he's seen in the industry and emphasized how important it is for auto mechanics to keep up with new technology and adapt to change. "It's not the same occupation that I grew up in, where you were known as a mechanic or a grease monkey. Now, you're just sitting in a car's seat with a laptop figuring out what's wrong with these cars."

Understandably, some auto mechanics are nervous about the future of the industry, considering all the advancements in vehicle technology. With more and more EVs on the road, there are bound to be changes in store, and some of them may be detrimental to traditional auto mechanics. Unlike gas engines, electric engines don't require oil changes and have fewer parts to be repaired. What's more, many of these EVs can be serviced remotely by downloading updates or purchasing parts online, without the car owner even having to visit a mechanic.

Craig Van Batenburg, who began working as an auto mechanic in the seventies, is concerned about job losses in the industry. "People are freaking out," he said, in a 2017 interview with the *Washington Post*. "Ninety percent of our industry has done nothing—absolutely nothing to prepare. They just turn the hybrids and EVs away and say, 'We don't work on those cars, go back to Ford or Toyota.' The fear factor is huge."

However, Jeffrey Cox, vice president of the Automotive Maintenance and Repair Association, who was also interviewed by the *Washington Post*, believes that auto mechanics can thrive in this new era of EVs as long as they are willing to adapt to the changing times. "The auto technician of the future will need to become some combination of your company's IT support guy with a car-lover's mind, someone with the ability to change tires and operate diagnostic and scanning equipment to root out problems involving computer networks and data processing."

A BRIGHT NEW FUTURE

Vehicles are evolving to keep pace with a technologically advancing world, dwindling fuel supplies, and potential new energy sources. Highly skilled automotive technicians who not only can keep up with these changes, but also race ahead to understand what tomorrow's needs might be and how the new machines will work will be highly valued. Becoming an automotive technician gives you the chance to expand and hone your talents while improving the safety and drivability of each vehicle you work on. In addition, you get paid well for doing something you love and are great at. It's a win-win situation for everyone!

Glossary

ALTERNATIVE FUELS A fuel used for powering vehicles that is not gasoline. Examples include methanol, natural gas, and electricity.

AUTOMOTIVE Of or relating to motor vehicles.

AUTONOMOUS VEHICLE A vehicle that can drive itself using computerized technology and does not require a driver; also known as a self-driving vehicle.

AXLE A central shaft or bar that a vehicle's wheels revolve on.

DIAGNOSTIC TECHNICIAN A technician who focuses primarily on figuring out what the problem is.

DIESEL An internal combustion engine where air is compressed to a high temperature, igniting fuel spontaneously.

DRAIN PAN A pan used to catch used oil during an oil change.

DRIVABILITY The way that a car feels while driving; the degree to which it feels smooth and steady.

DRIVE TRAIN A series of parts that deliver power from the engine to the wheels of a vehicle.

EMISSIONS The production and discharge of a substance; motor vehicles emit carbon dioxide, which contributes to climate change.

ENGINE LUBRICATION The process of applying oil to an engine to make sure it is running smoothly.

EV (ELECTRIC VEHICLE) A vehicle that runs on electricity, rather than gasoline.

EXHAUST SYSTEM A system of piping that guides exhaust gases outside the vehicle.

FRONT END A vehicle's front-end assembly, which includes the steering and suspension.

HIGH-PERFORMANCE CAR A car that is designed to go especially fast.

HYBRID CAR A car that is powered by both gasoline and electricity.

IGNITION A system that ignites a fuel-air mixture in a vehicle's engine to make the engine start.

SPRAY BOOTH Pressure-controlled booths used to spray paint vehicles.

SUSPENSION The system that controls the friction between the tires and the road to provide good steering and handling.

TRANSMISSION The assembly of parts, including the gears, that transmit power from the engine to the axel; some vehicles have automatic transmissions and some have manual transmissions.

For More Information

Alliance of Automobile Manufacturers
803 7th Street NW, Suite 300
Washington, DC 20001
(202) 326-5500
Website: https://autoalliance.org
Facebook: @autoalliance
Twitter: @auto_alliance
The Alliance of Automobile Manufacturers is a leading advocate for the auto industry. The organization develops policies around new auto technologies and initiates dialogues with policy makers and other stakeholders.

Automotive Industries Association of Canada
180 Elgin Street, Suite 1400
Ottawa, ON K2P 2K3
Canada
(613) 728-5821; Toll free: (800) 808-2920
Website: https://www.aiacanada.com
Facebook and Twitter: @AIAofCanada
The Automotive Industries Association of Canada provides advocacy and resources for professionals in the Canadian auto industry.

Automotive Service Association (ASA)
8209 Mid Cities Boulevard
North Richland Hills, TX 76182
(817) 514-2900
Website: https://asashop.org
Instagram: @ASA_national
Facebook and Twitter: @ASAshop

The ASA provides trainings, events, and resources for professionals in the auto repair industry.

Bureau of Labor Statistics
Postal Square Building, 2 Massachusetts Avenue NE
Washington, DC 20212
(202) 691-5200
Website: https://www.bls.gov/home.htm
Twitter: @BLS_gov
The Bureau of Labor Statistics provides comprehensive information and statistics about all types of labor, including qualifications required for each profession and links to additional job information resources.

Global Automakers of Canada
1 Concorde Gate, Suite 701, Box 20
Toronto, ON M3C 3N6
Canada
(416) 595-8251
Website: http://www.globalautomakers.ca
Global Automakers of Canada is an advocacy organization representing the policy interests of its members in the Canadian auto industry.

National Institute for Automotive Service Excellence (ASE)
1503 Edwards Ferry Road NE, Suite 401
Leesburg, VA 20176
(703) 669-6609
Website: https://www.ase.com/Home.aspx
Facebook and Twitter: @ASEtests

The ASE is a national nonprofit organization that aims to raise the standards of automotive care and repair by providing tests for professionals in all areas of auto mechanics. Most employers require technicians to have ASE certification.

Society of Automotive Engineers (SAE)
400 Commonwealth Drive
Warrendale, PA 15096
(724) 776-4841
Website: https://www.sae.org
Facebook: @SAEInternational
Twitter: @SAEIntl
SAE provides educational resources for professionals in the auto industry. The website includes links to a wide range of trade publications, including books and journals, as well as information about conferences and other industry events.

For Further Reading

Banks, Patrice. *Girls Auto Clinic Glove Box Guide.* New York, NY: Touchstone, 2017.

Clark, John. *The Basics of Mechanics.* New York, NY: Rosen Publishing, 2015.

Craig, Joe. *The Vo-Tech Guide to Success in Manufacturing, Mechanics, and Automotive Care.* New York, NY: Rosen Publishing, 2014.

Culp, Jennifer. *A Career as a Diesel Mechanic.* New York, NY: Rosen Publishing, 2019.

Kamberg, Mary-Lane. *Working as a Mechanic in Your Community.* New York, NY: Rosen Publishing, 2016.

Knowles, Don, and Bob Rodriguez. *Automotive Technician Certification Test Preparation Manual.* New York, NY: Clifton Park, 2013.

Miller, Malinda. *Modern Mechanics: Maintaining Tomorrow's Green Vehicles.* Broomall, PA: Mason Crest Publishers, 2014.

Mozer, Mindy. *Getting a Job in Automotive Care and Service.* New York, NY: Rosen Publishing, 2013.

Sclar, Deanna. *Automotive Repair for Dummies.* Hoboken, NJ: John Wiley & Sons, 2013.

Stribling, Dave. *The Complete Idiot's Guide to Auto Repair and Maintenance.* New York, NY: Alpha Books, 2015.

Bibliography

Automotive Schools. "Automotive Resources." Retrieved September 8, 2018. http://automotiveschools.com/resources.

Automotive Schools. "Degrees in Automotive." Retrieved September 8, 2018. http://automotiveschools.com/resources/degrees-in-automotive.

Automotive Schools. "Top 10 Qualities of a Great Auto Mechanic." Retrieved September 8, 2018. http://automotiveschools.com/resources/top-10-qualities-of-a-great-auto-mechanic.

Bureau of Labor Statistics. "Automotive Service Technicians and Mechanics." April 13, 2018. https://www.bls.gov/ooh/installation-maintenance-and-repair/automotive-service-technicians-and-mechanics.htm#tab-1.

Dr. Kit. "Career Video: Auto Body Technician." April 7, 2014. http://www.drkit.org/automotivebodytech.

Girls Auto Clinic. "About Girls Auto Clinic." Retrieved September 8, 2018. https://girlsautoclinic.com/aboutgac.

Green, Adrienne. "A Mechanic Faces the Age of the Self-Driving Car." *The Atlantic*, October 5, 2016. https://www.theatlantic.com/business/archive/2016/10/auto-mechanic-technician/502976.

Gross, Terri. "Girls Auto Clinic Owner: 'I Couldn't Find a Female Mechanic, So I Had to Learn.'" NPR, January 9, 2018. https://www.npr.org/2018/01/09/576747854/girls-auto-clinic-owner-i-couldnt-find-a-female-mechanic-so-i-had-to-learn.

Holley, Peter. "'People Are Freaking Out.' Will Electric Vehicles Doom Your Neighborhood Mechanic?'" *Washington Post*, December 11, 2017. https://www.washingtonpost.com/news/innovations/wp/2017/12/11/people-are-freaking-out-why-electric-vehicles-might-doom-your-neighborhood-auto-mechanic/?utm_term=.c01c9849aa8d.

Jacobsen, Art. Interview with Tamra Orr via email. September 26, 2009.

Johnson, Beau. "Guide to an Online Automotive Education." Automotive Schools. Retrieved September 8, 2018. http://automotiveschools.com/resources/guide-to-an-online-automotive-education.

Learn How to Become. "How to Become a Mechanic." Retrieved September 8, 2018. https://www.learnhowtobecome.org/mechanic.

Linton, Ian. "Types of Auto Mechanics." Chron.com. Retrieved September 8, 2018. https://work.chron.com/types-auto-mechanics-14127.html.

Mayersohn, Norman. "Shortage of Auto Mechanics Has Dealerships Taking Action." *New York Times*, April 27, 2017. https://www.nytimes.com/2017/04/27/automobiles/wheels/automobile-repair-jobs.html.

Mohr, B. Scott. "Hall of Fame Diagnostic Technician." *The Southsider Voice*, May 16, 2018. https://www.southsidervoice.com/top-stories/hall-of-fame-diagnostic-technician.

My Perfect Resume. "Auto Mechanic Job, Salary, and School Information." Retrieved September 8, 2018.

https://www.myperfectresume.com/how-to/career-resources/auto-mechanics.

National Institute for Automotive Service Excellence (ASE). "ASE Collision Repair and Refinish Tests: The Official ASE Study Guide." 2017. https://www.ase.com/MediaLibrary/Images/PDF%20folder/collision_guide.pdf.

NBC Nightly News. "How an All-Female Pennsylvania Car Repair Shop Is Defying Gender Stereotypes." January 23, 2017. https://www.youtube.com/watch?v=PWrPA1NMM9I.

Sivak, Cathy. "An Interview with Automotive Technician and Course Instructor, Michele Winn." Automotive Schools. Retrieved September 8, 2018. http://allautomotiveschools.com/resources/an-interview-with-automotive-technician-and-course-instructor-michele-winn.

Index

ABOUT THE AUTHORS

Rachel Given-Wilson has written and edited a number of nonfiction books for teenagers, including the Tech Girls series of books about careers for girls in STEM industries. She lives in Brooklyn with her family.

Tamra B. Orr is the author of books for young readers, including many titles relating to science, technology, and careers. She has won several awards for her books. Orr loves being a writer because it gives her a chance to learn more about the world every day. She lives in the Pacific Northwest with her husband, children, cat, and dog.

PHOTO CREDITS

Cover LightField Studios/Shutterstock.com; back cover, pp. 6–7, interior pages (background) Vixit/Shutterstock.com; p. 7 (inset) Jupiterimages/Stockbyte/Getty Images; p. 12 ElevenStudio /Shutterstock.com; p. 15 SaMBa/Shutterstock.com; p. 18 Ken Wolter/Shutterstock.com; p. 23 Kurhan/Shutterstock.com; p. 27 Happycreator/Shutterstock.com; p. 29 Joseph Sohm /Shutterstock.com; p. 33 kryzhov/Shutterstock.com; p. 35 CTR Photos/Shutterstock.com; p. 39 Vereshchagin Dmitry /Shutterstock.com; p. 42 Robert Crum/Shutterstock.com; p. 46 new person/Shutterstock.com; p. 49 JohnnyGreig/E+ /Getty Images; p. 52 Dmitry Kalinovsky/Shutterstock.com; p. 53 Action Sport Photography/Shutterstock.com; p. 57 welcomia /Shutterstock.com;p. 60 Bloomberg/Getty Images; p. 63 Ari N/Shutterstock.com; p. 64 Mike Flippo/Shutterstock.com.

Design and Layout: Nicole Russo-Duca; Photo Researcher: Sherri Jackson